MW01254678

# Gringo in Brazil

## Quick Guide for Enjoying Brazil on Your First Trip Plus a Little Portuguese the Easy Way

Written by JF Lewis

Published by Needed Knowledge, LLC

# INTRODUCTION

Exploring the beaches and cities of Brazil was absolutely wonderful and I highly recommend the adventure. For my preparation, I learned a few Portuguese words and phrases and read several books on traveling to this amazing country. When I stepped out of the resort I discovered my studies had fallen woefully short for the reality I found.

Brazil for me was more like visiting another planet, not country. It was extremely beautiful, exciting, fun, surprising and full of friendly people, but I also found it strange, complicated, dirty and even a little scary at times. Most fears could have been avoided if I had only known a little more. This book will improve your comfort and confidence, but if you have never traveled to South America, I do recommend using a guide to handle the driving or at least for the first few days of your visit.

My guide was a beautiful and sexy Brazilian. She taught me so many things, some of which I will share in this book. Our tips and experiences will help you know what to expect and not and most importantly how to stay safe and have a marvelous time on your very first trip to Brazil. Plan enough time to enjoy several of their beaches and the crystal clear refreshing ocean you will find there.

# TABLE OF CONTENTS

# LEGAL NOTES

The information contained herein is based on the author's experiences and knowledge from his life and travels. Although he makes every effort to be accurate, the statements and information contained herein are only his opinions.

He is not a lawyer and he is not providing legal advice or recommendations. This book is intended to be entertaining and informative for those wishing to visit Brazil. The author has taken only a few small poetic liberties for entertainment purposes.

This book contains the information he shares with his family and friends and hopes it will help you and yours. He provides his opinion on how to visit Brazil safer and what to expect when you arrive.

# CHAPTER 1
# WORDS TO GET YOU AROUND

## THE BASICS AND A LITTLE MORE

I admit my language skills (even English) are pitiful. That being said, you will notice that I use a few odd techniques (and thoughts) for attempting to remember words and sounds. I will choose words that are easier for me to pronounce and remember, but as you learn you may find others that fit you better.

While practicing my Portuguese I realized that it could take me decades to sound somewhat like a Brazilian and that I may never be able to make the sounds needed to do so. The ones that remind me of a cat spitting up his hair ball are especially difficult to master. My goal in this chapter is to provide you with quick and simple communications skills. You will find that most Brazilians appreciate your efforts to learn their language and will try to understand you so don't be too shy to speak. Not all, but many Brazilians also speak good English so you can normally throw in a couple English words if get stuck. If learning Portuguese isn't for you, then please jump right ahead to chapter two.

As you go through my tips and sounds for pronunciation, try not to hurt yourself laughing too hard and don't say I didn't warn you. My examples will not be 100% grammatically correct, but instead be shown as I in vision them sounding and in a way that I can remember them. As with all countries there are regional accents so you will find slight difference as you travel to various cities. The Chee sounds may become Ghee sounds. The throaty or rolling R sounds soften or become harsher, the cat sounds get louder and many others. These pronunciations are a combination of my guide's accent and my inability to reproduce those sounds or at least without spitting on everyone.

My Portuguese is very limited so no doubt I will make a few errors, but hopefully nothing that will slow down your fun in Brazil. In addition, many Portuguese words are gender specific and I will continue to make mistakes with those as well. Just think car or in Portuguese carro (car hoe) is considered masculine and a toaster or in Portuguese tosdaderia (toas tah day rah) is feminine. I will try to keep it very simple and if we forget the gender of the blender, oh well as long as our margarita or in Brazil, our caipirinha (cai phria hin yah, the Brazilian drink made from sugarcane that is similar to a margarita) is great.

Try to remember that O's at the end of words are typically masculine and A's are normally feminine. They frequently have to do with whether the speaker is a man or woman, but sometimes are related to an item. It can be very confusing and I will not spend a lot of time or effort on it in this book, just the basics.

Remember our goal is for quick and simple communications, even if it is somewhat butchered or uses the wrong gender. I want you to be able to order a coconut water, cold beer, dinner, ask for the check, find the bathroom or hotel, go shopping or to the beach and have some friendly basic conversations in broken Portuguese without much worry on your part.

As you attempt to speak gringo Portuguese, don't worry about a little spitting or attracting stray cats. If you do both of those, your Portuguese will most likely be better than mine. Enough said, let's get with it and get you on your way.

**First words to learn:**

Nao (nom, very light m sound) No

Sim (sim, like your phone sim card) Yes

Pouco (poo coo) little, small

Pouquinho (pee kene yho) little, small, even more so than Pouco, like my Portuguese

Grande (grand a) large, big

Muito (moe went toe) many, a lot

Bom (bon, light n sound) good

Mau (mal, silent u, rhymes with cow) bad

Por favor (poor fa vor) please

Desculpa (de scoup ia) excuss me

Cuidado (cou dah dough) caution

Eu (ee you) I

Voce (vo say) you

Nos (noh sa) we

Este (s tey) this

Este e (s tey e) this is

Estes (s tey es) these

Estes sao (s tey es somn) these are

Gostar (goo sta, silent r) like

Amor (a more) love

Beijo (bay joe) kiss

Nao gosto (nom goo stoe, light m) dislike

Mais (mia za) more

Menos (may nose) less

Mais ou menos (mia za o may nose) more or less

Rapido (ha pee dough) fast

Divagar (de vah ga) slow

Claro (clar o) of course, evident, clear

Quem (cane or kain) who

que (o k) what

Quando (kwan doe) when

Onde (un day) where

Porque (pho kay) why

Como (comb oh) how

**Greetings:**

Oi (oy, boy without the b) hi or hello

Tchau (chow) bye or goodbye

Bom dia (bon dee ah) good morning

Boa tarde (boa tar dee) good afternoon

Boa noite (boa noy tee) good night

Qual e seu nome (kwa oh e see o nom ee) what is your name?

meu nome e ___(oh me oh nom ee eh___) my name is ____.

Tudo bom (to dough bon) How are you, is everything good, I am good, everything is well, exact same as tudo bem

Tudo bem (to dough bang, yes bang) How are you, is everything good, I am good, everything is well, exact same as saying tudo bom, but typically when asked tudo bom, you should say tudo bem and vice versa

Oi, tudo bem (oy or ohee, to dough bang) Hi, how are you

Adeus (ah dee osh or ah dee ooz) goodbye for a long time, where as Tchau is usually just for a little while

### Useful short sentences:

Um coco gelado por favor (um Coo co gah la doh poor fa vor) one extremely cold fresh coconut water in the shell.

I was amazed at how proficient the coconut merchants are with a machete. I saw one young lady about fifteen open a coconut with two full swings of her machete while holding the coconut in her other hand. The cut was so close to exposing the water that you only had to gently push your straw through the super thin membrane she left. I recommend strongly that you do not attempt this at home and do not piss off any coconut girls.

Mais uma (mia za um a) one more

A conta por favor (ah con tah poor fa vor) the check please. You can also use the international hand gesture of signing to get your check.

Nao entendi (nom inten dee, I remembered the word by associating it with the similar sounding game console name) I didn't understand or don't understand

Nao entendo Portugues eu falo Ingles (nom inten doh port a gaze e u follow eng las) I don't understand Portuguese. I speak English

Eu falo pouquinho Portugues (e u follow pee keen yho port a gaze) I speak little Portuguese

Como se fala _____ em Portugues (com o say fah la ____ aim port a gaze) how do you say ____ in Portuguese? Just insert the word you want to know how to say.

Um momento por favor (um mow men toe poor fa vor) one moment please

Por favor repita devagar (poor fa vor re pete tah dee vah gah) can you please repeat what you said slowly


**Directions:**

Pare (pah dee, almost party if said quickly with a soft t /d sound, close to potty with soft t) stop

Vai (vi, strong I sound) go

Direita (de ray tah) right

Esquerda (s ska dah) left

Em frente (in freen tee) straight or in front of

Aqui (ah key) here

Ali (ah lee) there

Por ali (poor ah lee) through there

Perto (pa exh toe, exh sounds like a cat with a hair ball) close

Longe (lon ghee) far


## People and places:

Senhor (sin your) Mr.

Senhora (sin your ah) Mrs.

Senhorita (sin your rita) Miss, young lady

Garcon (gar son) waiter

Amingo (ah mig go) friend

Filho (fill yoh) son

Filha (fill yah) daughter

Menino (ma nen oh) boy

Menina (ma nen ah) girl

Homen (ohm may, in between sounding like ohm me and ohm main) man

Mulher (mule yarh) woman

Gente boa (jan tah boa) good people

Banheiro (ban yhair oo) bathroom

Casa (ka sa) home

Bar (bah) bar

Restaurante (hes ta rhan te, r sound is often an h sound) restaurant

Sao Paulo (somn pa low) huge city southwest of Recife about three hours by jet, this city is like Brazil's New York.

Recife (he sif ee, r is h sound) a big city in the northeast of the country on the coast, like many cities there are dozens of neighborhoods or burros, bairro (bye hoe) Most of my new Brazilian friends live in or near Recife.

Boa Viagen (bo via ag ee, like bon voyage, good trip) A suburb or bairro of Recife.

Galinha (guy-lean-yah, remember a guy leaning) part of a beautiful beach city's name, Porto de Galinhas, chicken port, hen or female chicken.

Olinda (O lin dah) a coastal city north of Recife with a beautiful mountain view of the city and ocean. If you visit here, go explore the mountain top church, then have a fresh coconut water while you take in the view.

Rio Mar (rio mar) Rio mall

## Time and numbers:

Hoje (oh ghee) today

Agora (ah gore ah) now

Mais tarde (mia za tar dee) later

Que horas sao (kay or ahs somn) what time is it?

E uma hora da tarde (a um a or ah dah tar dee) it is one o clock in the afternoon.

Um (um) 1

Dois (doy ce ) 2

Tres (trace) 3

Quatro (qua trow) 4

Cinco (sink co) 5

Seis (say es) 6

Sete (sat tee) 7

Oito (Oi toe) 8

Nove (nah vee) 9

Dez (days) 10

Vinte (ven tee) 20

Trinta (trin ta) 30

Quarenta (quia en tah) 40

Cinquenta (sin quen tah) 50

Sessenta (sa sin tah) 60

Sententa (sa ten tah) 70

Oitenta (oi ten tah) 80

Noventa (no ven tah) 90

Cem (sain) 100

If you were checking out of a shop the clerk might say "E nove reais e trinta centravos (a nah vee hey eyes (plural of real, hey al) ee tren tah sin tah vohs) which translates to "Is nine reais (Brazilian dollars) and thirty cents.

Try starting with these words and phrases and then add a couple more each day of your trip. I do recommend using a translation application on your phone or at least a Portuguese dictionary to supplement these. The apps I have used are good for referencing words or checking pronunciation, but are too slow for use in a conversation. If you have any down time, try to watch the news or a Brazilian soap opera. You may be surprised how many new words you can pick up and Brazilians love their soaps.

# Chapter 2
# To Speak or Not to Speak

## What Not to Say and Things

There are inappropriate things you should not say and sometimes when it is best to say nothing at all. I would stay away from Portuguese words that if said slightly wrong can mean something entirely different or even be offensive. The only dangerous word I use frequently is "coco". Just make certain you put the emphasis on the first syllable or you will get some strange looks. It is best to practice new words with your guide or other Brazilian friend before trying them in public.

Whatever you do, do not give anyone the OK sign. It's a little worse than using the middle finger vigorously. You can say OK, it translates just fine and thumbs up or down is universal. If the OK sign slips, then quickly say "Me desculpe" (me dah scoo pee) which means I'm sorry or you can say "Me perdoe" (me pay ha do ee, almost a little cat sound in the middle of the pay and ha) which means pardon me. Of the two, perdoe is much harder for me to pronounce so I stick with desculpe.

Please remember to use caution with some words. In Portuguese there are words, whose meaning will be determined not just by their spelling, but also by the other words in the sentence. There are still other words that are pronounced so similar to others that I struggle with them and must speak "com cuidado" (con cou dah doe, with caution). The meaning of some words has more to do with which syllable to give emphasis or pronounce louder. Remember, I definitely recommend you either try these out with your guide or other Brazilian friend or at least hear and practice them with a translation app before using them with strangers. Here are just a few.

Coco (Coo co, first syllable is pronounced hardier) coconut

Coco (co Coo, second syllable is pronounced hardier) shit

Como (comb oo) why

Como (comb oo) to eat

Comer (comb may) eating

Coma (comb ma) unconscious

Perto (pa exh toe, exh is the best I could come with for the cat and hair ball sound) close

Parto (par exh toe) giving birth

Cem (sain) 100

Sem (sain) without

Sim (sim) yes

Sao (somn) whole, healthy, well balanced, are

Cafetao (ca phay toln) pimp

Café (ca pha) coffee

Porao (poa rhon, rolling r sound) basement

Porra (poa hah) semen, it is a cuss word used like
we say "shit" or "damm"

Vadiar (vah dia exh, cat hair ball sound) to lounge
around or wander

Vadia (vah dia) slut

     Deciding what to say or whether to speak at
all is worthy of a little consideration. You can easily
cross the wrong street and start feeling
uncomfortable. Many nice areas that you will visit in
Brazil are next to poor neighborhoods or even
favelas. Oddly for me, these areas were right next
door to wealthiest areas. They were next to the
mall, next to the beach, next to the restaurant, next
to the luxury high rise, next to everywhere I went.
The rich and the poor are not always as
geographically segregated as you find in other
countries like the U.S. I don't know if this is better
or worse or right or wrong, but it just is, in Brazil.
Unfortunately some of these areas have high crime
rates and can be dangerous.

There also seems to be a somewhat accepting culture for corruption and even flat out theft among the Brazilian people. The attitude almost seems to be you can steal from me, but only if you take a little. I was not able to determine if it was their history and culture or just a fact of life that goes along with the poverty and their government or something entirely different. They seem to have far fewer police and less concern with laws than I am accustomed to. In many areas their infrastructure appears to be behind the times or in need of repair.

The drug use; even with children is as bad or worse as it is in the U.S.'s inner cities. On one occasion I witnessed two small children sniffing glue out in the open right beside the road. I suspect this is caused for similar reasons in all cities of the world and it is just sad that it exists anywhere. Brazil does have a lot of social programs, welfare, a public health care system, many others like most developed nations and they continue to implement nationwide changes each year. Many things are changing in Brazil right now, but let's get back to the tourist stuff.

Gringos (tourist and especially Americans) seem to be viewed by the robbers as not only rich, but as easy targets. When you're not sure how safe an area is or you feel an area is high risk, simply try not to speak English or Portuguese. You may attract the wrong crowd. I am not trying to scare anyone off from visiting this great country and having their grand adventure, but just to do it safer. Many of these areas that seem dangerous are not, but it is best to err on the side of caution. Often it is just a poor neighborhood and not a favela. I will explain favelas more in chapter eight, but just know favelas are dangerous and if you're not sure, just stay out.

To avoid many problems while traveling and especially in Brazil you should attempt to blend in and not stand out. Don't wear your brand new anything. Wear your casual clothes and shoes and if they are a little faded, torn or frayed, even better. Don't carry a camera bag or designer purse, especially the big ones. Don't wear American designer name brand clothing with logos on display. Don't walk down the street taking pictures of everything or staring up at the architecture non-stop. Do not look like a tourist.

Whatever you choose to wear, don't wear your socks with sandals or other similar attire. It is not only a fashion mistake, but is certain to get you robbed or at least it should and every local will know you are a dumb gringo. However, if you put on a pair of flip flops (some say shower shoes) you will automatically become 20% Brazilian. If you select the famous Brazilian name brand that I won't mention, then you become 40% Brazilian or more.

As with anywhere you go, you should be aware of your surroundings and especially with the people that are paying attention to you. If you walk out of jewelry store in the mall and notice someone following you as you head to the exit, don't exit immediately. The malls have considerable security and it is very acceptable to ask for an escort through the parking garage. Another good option is simply to continue shopping or get something to eat or a coffee and see if your follower grows tired of waiting and leaves. These thieves typically are looking for someone easy to rob and who isn't paying any attention to them or their surroundings. Once they realize you are on to them, they often just go away. If you happen to walk up to security guard and ask which way to the bathroom (Por favor onde e o banheiro?) and start pointing, they will usually be gone before you turn around.

If you need to go to an ATM or bank, make sure it is in the daytime and with plenty of other people there. Never go to an ATM at night. Park your car close to the bank and pay attention to your surroundings. Many banks will even have secured parking, but you still need to pay attention and walk quickly. You also need to know that banks in Brazil almost always require you to go through a metal detector to enter. Many of these are through a bullet proof glass revolving door that will stop if you have something metal with you. This includes your phone, so leave it in the glove box or with a friend. They do have a little tray to pass your keys and coins through before you get in the revolving door.

Most do not allow phone use inside the bank even if you bring it in. The reasoning is that a bad guy could identify someone getting a large sum of money to the thieves waiting outside. If you deal with a person instead of a machine, they will likely write down amounts and not say the number so that others do not hear how much money you are withdrawing. Do not display a large sum of cash. Simply put it in your purse or pocket quickly. If you use a little common sense and these few tips, you should be fine.

I discovered that parts of the Brazilian education system were different than I expected. As I understand it, if you're family is poor or especially if they are extremely poor you will go to the public schools or not go to school at all sometimes. I have heard stories about how common this was in the U.S. on farms and in a few other situations that existed fifty plus years ago, but I had almost forgotten them. Today Brazil does not require all children to attend school. As with most countries, the public school system is not considered as good as the private schools. If your family can afford it, you will attend private school from your first days until college.

I further understand that when you finish high school you may attend free government college if you score well on the "Vestibular" test. This government test seems to determine your aptitude for a profession, along with everyone else who takes it that year. You are allowed to pick a first and second career choice. If you don't score well enough for your first choice, you may for your second choice. If your score is not high enough for either, you can retake the test next year.

This is quite different to today's U.S. school systems and choices, but maybe more practical and definitely more cost effective. I'm not advocating we change are system in the U.S., but I thought these education differences were interesting enough to mention. That's not what this book is really about so let's move on.

# CHAPTER 3
# WHAT TO TAKE AND WHY

## PERFECT PACKING

I always recommend taking a small carry on with two or three days worth of clothing, your toiletry bag, spare glasses and sunglasses, copies of your passport, visa, drivers license, itinerary, credit cards you carry, tickets medicines and other important documents. In addition to these hard copies, email photos of these to your email. That way if things get lost or stolen you can simply print them out again. Don't forget that you may need to interview for a visa in person, but you can check on line to find out and start the application. I did my interview in Miami and my visa was emailed to me in about two weeks or less. You may also want to carry a small amount of insect repellent and sun screen. You definitely want to pack plenty of both of these in your checked luggage. The mosquitoes were fairly bad at night if you were not near the ocean. The good news is the repellent we used worked fantastically and the sun screen as well. I like to put several packages of nuts or small snacks in my carry-on bag and a book to pass the time with when you're just waiting.

Another reason to take this small carry-on bag is so that your checked baggage actually arrives at your destination with you. If you don't take it, your checked baggage may not arrive intact or not for a couple days or not at all. A small back pack is perfect for this job. Don't tempt fate; it will bite you in the bunda (boon dah, butt). Be a boy scout, take the carry-on and be prepared.

I recommend having a small amount of cash from both your home country and the country you are traveling to. This will help with any emergencies and be super convenient for small food and beverage purchases and also for tipping the guy who helps you with your luggage. The cash will also give you something easy to hand over if you're mugged. You need know to take small bills to places like the beach or small local shops that often cannot provide change for anything over 20 reais (hey eyes, the plural of real, hey al). While discussing cash, please note a few gas stations will not take credit cards and a fill up can easily cost 100 reais.

As far as your checked bags go, confirm with the airline the number of bags you can take without additional charges and the maximum weights. Before you leave your home, weigh your bags. It is much easier to move things around or leave items behind when this is done at home. I recommend not only putting address cards in and on your bags, but also to add something unique and colorful to them. Later when you are trying to find them on the baggage carousel, you will be happy that the bright yellow ribbon is tied to your handles. Depending on your type and shape of bags, a brightly colored belt around the middle of it can not only guarantee your contents arrive with your bag, but it sure does make it easier to spot your bags on the carousel. Take as many bags as they allow so that you can bring home some goodies. If you are like me you will find plenty of handmade crafts or art to bring home and a few good bags of coffee are a must. I was amazed at how inexpensive many of the local handcrafted items were.

A good tip for shopping in Brazil is that most every price is negotiable, especially when paying with reais or even US dollars. Just be careful about using US dollars in some places. If you're not sure how safe the area is, don't use US dollars or other foreign currencies. It may bring unwanted attention or thieves around once they consider you a rich tourist.

# CHAPTER 4
# EATS AND COLD DRINKS

## CHURRASCO, WATER, BEER, WINE AND SPIRITS

Churrasco (shoe rhos co, grilled or barbecued meat) or bife (be ifh, beef) is wonderful in Brazil. Your servers wonder by your table with various skewers of different meats cooked to various temperatures. I prefer the picanha and filet cuts cooked medium rare. They will shave off as many pieces as you wish onto your side dish. You may need to assist them with your tongs if they hesitate cutting the slice completely. The tongs come on your side dish. I highly recommend you try the feijoada (phash wah dah, a black bean soup loaded with pork meats and sausages) as well. It is a traditional Brazilian dish that is not only richly flavored, but extremely hearty and filling.

The fruits are amazing not only in flavor, but also the sheer variety you will find. It is not uncommon to see fruit trees growing everywhere. While you wonder around, be very cautious not to walk under a Jack Fruit tree. These trees are huge shade trees, maybe as tall as eighty feet. The Jack Fruit that grows in them is about the size of a water melon with huge two inch hard spikes on the outside. Needless to say, if you unlucky enough to have one fall on you, it could be fatal. If it were not fatal, it would definitely leave a hell of a mark.

There are not only a great number of restaurants, but many types of restaurants to be found. I enjoyed many different dishes in many places. A few of my favorites were surprisingly at the mall and of course on and in the ocean. It doesn't seem fair to go into detail about the day we were lucky enough to spend with friends on a huge yacht, so I will not. I will say the fresh seafood and adult beverages we had on that day, on and in the ocean were divine and a great time was had by all.

The only ones I would not advise trying are the street vendors and the beach vendors. They are great for cold fresh coconut water or beer and I am sure most of them are wonderful period, but I was just unwilling to take a chance on stomach problems during my vacation. We did find many small places tucked away that where absolutely amazing and a few odd ones that we enjoyed as well. One restaurant we visited a few times sold their food by the pound or actually by the kilogram. It's a neat concept that is great if you are trying to eat small amounts and save money at the same time. It is like the opposite of all you can eat buffets and the freshness was out of this world. This was one of the few places we found that served a great salad every time.

In a few of the restaurants we ate we were given a card as we entered or were seated. These cards were used to keep up with the amount of food and beverages you consumed. When you have finished your meal, you use this card to pay up and gain your freedom out the door. A few of the places had someone to take your card after you paid and open door and others had a turnstile type exit that you must put your card into to exit.

At some street side bars and restaurants they will simply leave the empty bottles on the table or line them up on the floor. That way they can make an accurate count when you're ready to close out your check. Others will leave a slip of paper on your table to keep count of the cold beers so don't be surprised as they lean over your table to update it when they deliver the next one.

The tap water in Brazil is to bath in and not good to drink. Most houses, condos and apartments will have a water cooler in them for drinking water. You will see delivery men on bicycles all around town loaded with hundreds of pounds of water weaving in and out of traffic. When you are out on the town if you do want water, always get bottled water. If possible select a brand that you have had before. Not all bottled water tastes the same (nudge, nudge, wink, wink). I prefer com gas (carbonated or with gas). If you don't, then ask for agua sem gas (water without gas). I'm not sure how safe the ice or gelo (gel low) is, but if you cover it in Vodka or Scotch; I think you will be fine.

The beer however is among the best that I have ever had. I remember coming back from Europe several years ago and telling all my friends about the wonderful beers I drank. The beers in Brazil during the summer were equivalent to those or superior or the combination of the warm air and cold beer were. Brazilians take cold beer (Cerveja, bottled or chopp, draft beer) to a new level. If you are like me you will find yourself drinking ice cold beer frequently. When ordering a beer you say "Cerveja (the brand you prefer) super gelada (say vah gha souper gah la dah) and if it is not a couple degrees above freezing or colder, it is quite acceptable to send it back for one that is. If you have a guest with you, you may wish to say dois copos por favor (doyce call pulls poor fa vor, two glasses please). They often serve a large bottle of beer with small, maybe eight or ten once glasses.

When you order a drink such as vodka or scotch, they may bring the bottle. It made me think of the old westerns where the cowboys would say "leave the bottle" to the bartender. Make sure to check the level of liquor when you start and finish. They often have it marked on a label that is pasted to the side of the bottle, but not always. They normally present the gelo (gel low, ice) and mixers on the side.

I enjoy wine, but I only had wine a couple times during my trip. It is only served by the bottle so if you just want a glass or two, it doesn't make sense. Another downside to wine (vee know) in Brazil is the cost as compared to the U.S. It is a little more than double even after the great exchange rate we enjoyed. I believe most of their wine is imported so that's probably why the cost is high. The final reason not to drink wine in Brazil is the super warm climate and the ice cold fabulous beer you will find everywhere. If you really enjoy wine, get some at the duty free shop on your way in.

# CHAPTER 5
# CRAZY CARS AND INSANE BIKES

## TRAFFIC AND PARKING

I strongly recommend not driving a car in Brazil unless you have nerves of steel, quick reflexes, good insurance and zero issues with road rage. Foreigners are legally allowed to drive with a valid foreign driver's license, but I urge against it or at least for the first few days. It is best if you have a guide or local friend handle the driving. If you take a motorcycle ride you will confirm without any doubt that you have completely lost your mind. What you will witness cars, trucks, busses and especially motorcycles do goes well beyond my ability to describe. Saying it is crazy and insane is the best I can do, but it is an extremely lacking description.

It appears that Brazilians don't really have traffic laws, but instead sort of have traffic suggestions for day light hours. Lanes are rarely keep to and traffic lights don't count after dark (I was told it is not safe to stop your car at night). If people in front of you completely stop at a light, instead of just slowing down, leave some room between their car and yours. To change lanes or merge, you just cut someone off. During the daytime if you leave any room between you and the next vehicle, it is basically an invitation for another car, truck or motorcycle to cut you off. If you hesitate merging into traffic (i.e. cutting someone off immediately) you will hear from the other cars behind you. They have only one rock solid traffic law that is strongly enforced. That law is zero tolerance of drinking and driving. They check for this by running huge road blocks at night that they call "Blitz". I have heard of some locals getting out of a fine with a good sized bribe, but I am not sure if that is true or how successful a gringo would be. So if you drink, let someone else drive. Remember they do not have an acceptable level of alcohol in your system. Any amount will get you arrested and likely mess up an otherwise great vacation.

Traffic can be ridiculous by anyone's standards and it can take hours to cross town at the wrong time. I'm certain this is one of the reasons for the large number of motorcycles you will find in Brazilian cities. Often it will appear that half of the vehicles on the road are motorcycles. When the cars and trucks are grid locked, they continue on with little delay and at times quickly. They go around, between and sometimes over or through anything in their way.

I recommend driving around with the windows up and doors locked for security and the air conditioner on high so you don't melt. If you do hang your arm out of the window, be cautious. I was told that thieves on motorcycles will grab watches as they drive by so you may want to switch the hand you wear your watch on. In addition, when you stop with your window down you are an easier target for robbers. Another reason not to is the possible injury caused by a wreck or the motorcycles that are always flying by.

After just a few days in Brazil, I started asking myself why there are so many people missing arms and legs. I initially thought this was from the sharks (one of my big fears) that are reportedly bad near Recife. After experiencing the driving styles, I was not surprised to hear from local doctors instead it was mainly due to the frequent motorcycle wrecks. Please be safe and just keep the windows up and your doors locked.

In the cities and neighborhoods I visited parking was considerable different than what I was accustomed to. It was not uncommon to double or triple park. We even parked on the sidewalk if no other spot were available. Remember their traffic laws are mostly just suggestions and are not taken very seriously. More times than not when you pull into a parking spot on the street you will quickly be greeted by someone who advises he will watch your car. He will hold traffic for you to park and even let you know how much further you can back up before hitting the other car.

There will not be a meter to pay, but it is customary to give your attendant a couple reais (hey al, Brazilian money) when you leave. When I visited the exchange rate was over three point five to one so the two reais was less than sixty cents U.S. That's pretty cheap parking to me. If you leave in the daytime, he will remove the shade giving cardboard from your front windshield and stop traffic for you to pull out. Although they can seem a little forceful, especially if competing with another attendant, I actually liked them helping us park.

One last caution about parking, do not leave anything of value visible in your car. Remember there are a lot of very poor people in Brazil and making things even more tempting is just wrong. Do them and yourselves a favor and put the camera in the trunk when you leave the countryside and before you park at the restaurant. Put your phone or wallet under the floor mats when you leave them in the car.

# CHAPTER 6
# MASS TRANSIT AND
# PERSONAL SPACE

## GETTING AROUND TOWN AND A
## COUPLE TIDBITS

In Sao Palo we decided to explore the city for a day. We took the bus during rush hour traffic and after a bit of delay we finally made it to the train station. My guide told me the traffic in Sao Paulo can seem like rush hour all day long so there is no point in waiting to start a trip there. I was cautioned to keep anything important in my front pockets. As I understand it, the pick pockets are very active on mass transit, especially with the zero amount of personal space given.

It is important to realize in Brazil the lack of personal space that Americans are use to doesn't exist. In Brazil it is not abnormal or wrong in any way to be touching a stranger if you are on the bus or in a line. They actually have a negative amount of personal space. It is not uncommon to even feel a little pressure against you. Their culture does not allow for an inch of space, let alone feet like you may be use to. If you mingle with the masses, you will be pushed on a little and leaned on occasionally. So when it happens, try not to be offended or respond harshly. A Brazilian saying about personal space on the bus goes something like "You may get pregnant on the bus and not even know who the father is". It doesn't translate great, but you get the point. On the other side of the coin, a kiss on both cheeks is a common greeting among friends in Brazil and then there's the great weather, marvelous food, beer, coconuts, super clear ocean water, beaches and tiny bathing suits. When in Rome, do as the Romans do or at least to the extent you feel comfortable.

We then proceeded to catch a couple trains and walk the sidewalks of Sao Paulo. Their train system was pretty nice, clean and relatively easy to use. In Sao Paulo we found many nice shops to patronize and a couple great restaurants as well. I should remind you to wear walking shoes when undergoing these type adventures and run when crossing the streets. Pedestrians do not have the same rights as you might be used to. Don't expect the cars, motorcycles or even bicycles to slow down or stop for you. You really have to look out for the motorcycles, especially when the cars are stopped.

After a wonderful day, we retraced our footsteps, two trains and a bus and returned to our destination without issue. I am giving you the same cautions I was provided, but please don't let them stop you from getting out and exploring. Exploring Brazil is an experience everyone should have and you may never be the same afterwards. It is simply great fun and a huge adventure. Visiting Brazil changed me in too many ways to say.

A few other tidbits to go over start with safe swimming and the banheiro (ban yhair oo). High tide swimming or swimming in the open ocean is risky to say the least. I do not recommend it at all. You will see plenty of freshly painted sighs to remind you about the sharks. Recife in particular has a bad reputation for them. On the other hand, many beaches where I visited had huge natural reefs just off shore. At low tide these natural pools would appear and with the clear water you could see everything you would be swimming with. These natural pools are a great place to snorkel or just relax. They are beautiful and the water temperature is perfect. Admittedly I was only able to visit a few beaches during my trip, but my favorite at this point is Porto de Galinhas. I think it was just a little over an hour south of Recife by car.

Let's move onto the bathroom or banheiro. In most places in Brazil, you do not put your used toilet paper in the toilets. The banheiro will always have a small trash can near the toilet for this. Their plumbing will not handle it so don't forget. You will likely overflow the toilet if you do.

You will frequently not find a hot water knob on the sink or in the shower. The good news is that you won't need it. The water will typically be warm and the air temperature HOT. Some showers will have an electric hot water heater mounted on the shower head, but mixing 220 volt electricity and water in my shower gave me too much cause for concern. I spent a couple days at a resort that did have solar hot water, but first thing in the morning it didn't do much. Again, it really wasn't that necessary and I adjusted to it swiftly. Being cool in Brazil is generally considered absolutely wonderful.

If you get the chance to visit Rio Mar in Recife, do it. The mall there is not like a normal American mall. It is the largest and nicest mall that I have ever visited. I have had many mall visits and experiences in the U.S. The nicest and largest I had ever been in was about one quarter the size of the Rio Mar and none compared to the Rio Mar. This thing is huge, beautiful, multifaceted, and modern and even has a heliport on top. The mall experience here is unlike any I have ever had. It is an event to go to the mall and you can easily spend the day before you know it. If you want to buy groceries or a beach front condo while you're there, you can. As you would expect by your reading so far, it is of course surrounded on all sides by the local favela which also happens to be one of the most dangerous in the area. The contrasts like this are often found in Brazil. They are strange to a gringo, but they may even make the nice things nicer.

I started not to include the next paragraph about the beaches and swim suit styles, but I just couldn't stop myself. When you travel to the beaches in Brazil, you will see things that you have never seen before. Most of them will be delightful, some amusing and a couple frightening. You will find fit young men and women with extremely small bikinis on and you will find very mature and quite heavy men and women wearing the same bathing suit styles proudly.

A believe it was a doctor friend who told us a little joke that went something like "we call the super small thong bikinis "floss bikinis" because they go places that only floss can reach, but now women are wearing "mouthwash bikinis". Mouthwash goes places even floss cannot". It sounds somewhat sexy, interesting or at least funny until you see it on a mature large person, then it is not. There are actually things in this world you don't want to see or know, so please "cuidado" and especially if you have inquisitive children with you. I observed one large lady that from twenty yards away you absolutely could not tell if she was wearing a bathing suit or not. You have been warned so govern yourself accordingly.

You will see merchants on the beach selling everything. They are not just selling food and beer, but just about anything you can imagine. Some of the carts you will see being rolled down the beach are huge. Enjoy your day at the beach, swim at low tide and be prepared to close your eyes at times. One more thing, take sun screen, a hat and long sleeves. The Brazilian sun can feel like a laser and it will hurt you if you don't protect yourself.

# CHAPTER 7
# MONEY, MORE OR LESS

## CASH, CREDIT ATMS AND BANKS

The scariest thing I witnessed while on my trip to Brazil was not at the beach or driving through a Favela, but instead being near banks and armored cars at the wrong time. The wrong time is when cash is being moved. Normally you will see five or more heavily armed guards with body armor on. They will have their weapons drawn or at least half drawn and some will have their fingers on the triggers.

I was swept (that means a gun was pointed directly at me) more than once from a twelve gauge shotgun by guards who seemed willing and ready to kill. They had their heads on a pivot, guns ready and you could feel and almost taste the fear in the air. Their extreme focus and serious demeanor lead me to believe that robbing armored cars or even banks must not be that uncommon. Their jobs were obviously very dangerous and I did not like being near them or the potential gunfight. Afterwards I started leaving the area immediately when I would see these guys coming to pick up or deliver cash.

Surprisingly regular police on their motorcycles, walking in the malls or down the city streets often had a holster on, but no gun in it. I once witnessed 5 officers standing together with only one officer carrying a pistol. They normally just had a club. As we drove around I also noticed that police even with their lights on were not given much if any special consideration. It was just something way different for me, but normal in Brazil.

Let's talk a second about your credit cards. Before you leave for your trip to Brazil, I recommend you check your credit cards and take the ones that have little or no international fees associated with them. Call those credit card companies and make sure they know you will be traveling and what dates. Then use your credit cards for everything over a few reais. This will keep your need to visit banks or ATMs to a minimum and it is just easier. We went to the bank twice while in Brazil. Both of our visits took a long time. You will find that many things in Brazil take longer than you may be use to so slow down. Try to simply accept it and find something pleasant to do or think about while you wait. The Brazilian culture is a little slower than the American culture.

When you pay at a restaurant with a card, you will notice they do not take your credit card with them ever. They will bring the credit card machine to your table. If not, you will walk over to the register and use your credit card there. This same procedure will occur everywhere including the full service gas stations. They will either bring the machine to you or you will go to their machine, but you will never let anyone leave with your credit card. I am not sure if it is normal or not, but I did not have any credit card problems or fraud during my last two week trip.

Almost always a tip or service fee will already be added to the check. It is normally about ten percent and additional tipping is not normal. A few times I did, but it mainly just caused confusion. I was also asked by a local not to tip extra because he would have to live with the inflation I created long after I had returned to America. The only successful tip I was able to leave was by placing the exact amount of cash for the bill in one direction and a few more reais in another. Do what makes you happy, but you will blend in better if you don't tip extra.

# CHAPTER 8
# CRIME AND THE FAVELAS

## THE TRUTH ABOUT BRAZIL

As I stated earlier in this book, many areas are home to people living in poverty. These areas frequently have high crime rates and you are subject to be robbed, especially if you're a gringo. In addition, drug use is just as bad as or even worse than other countries I have visited. I didn't witness any robberies, but they do occur many times a day in most Brazilian cities.

At a glance most gringos simply can't tell the difference between poor communities and favelas. Unlike some poor neighborhoods, favelas are usually made by squatters that didn't purchase, lease or rent the land or house they live in. Typically they build with zero plans or infrastructure and definitely no inspectors.

These favelas are often occupied in part by gangs and drug dealers, but there are also regular people and families just doing the best they can. Normally there is little to no police presence or protection. In some of the worst areas of the favelas, the police will not go without a large heavily armed group. These same types of areas exist most everywhere in the world, but the favelas just seemed vastly different at first glance to me. They were cities unto themselves.

As I understand they are self governed shanty towns that are run by a different and violent set of rules. They are much more dangerous than a normal neighborhood even for a Brazilian. I am sure that I don't fully understand favelas and that part of what I have written is not correct and there are exceptions always, but that's what I took away from my experience. I was warned about them from my guide and I would simply not recommend a gringo visit one on their vacation.

I now have many Brazilian friends with greatly varying backgrounds, educations and careers. They range from doctors to grocery delivery men and everywhere in-between. I know a sweet old man who delivers groceries and water by bicycle. He also walks dogs and does other small jobs to make his living. He's an interesting person who never went to school a day and cannot read or write, but seems willing to help anyone in need. I know another man who has more than one college degree, worked on oil rigs in the ocean in his youth and now runs a very successful and huge business. I know a lawyer who is studying to be a Judge and another who is still in school to become an architect. I know so many doctors and one writer. One of my friends ran a heavy machinery rental company for years and now manages a few full service gas stations. They still have full service gas stations (only thirty percent of them or less are self service) in Brazil. You choose gasoline or alcohol, not the octane number, so you need to know which one to use in your car. The alcohol is cheaper, but both are expensive compared to the U.S. At full service stations you do not pump your own gas or even get out of the car. Before an honest attendant starts filling up your car they will want you to look at the pump to show you that they have reset it and are starting from zero. Some less honest ones might fill up a motorcycle and then your car without ever resetting the pump.

I love full service gas stations, but let's get back to crime. During my two week visit, one of my friend's gas stations was robbed twice. Both times two men on a motorcycle rode up with tinted visors on their helmets and a pistol and robbed all the men working there. The robbers then simply rode off down the street in rush hour traffic. My guide recounted a couple times she was robbed including while she was in a gift store shopping. The robbers entered, took everyone's money, jewelry, phones, wallets purses and then locked everyone in a closet and left.

I have heard other stories of drugged children using forks held to a person's neck to rob them. I have heard of children lying in the road so you will stop and when you do, you are robbed. I have no idea how frequent these robberies are, but it seems it is just part of the way of life in many

Brazilian cities. Be careful just as you would if you were in L.A., New Your, Chicago, Philadelphia, Miami or Atlanta. The Brazilian robbery stories I hear almost never have anyone resisting and rarely is anyone injured. It seems most people carry a little bit to give to the robbers and either don't carry much more or hide the rest of it. Most of the time the robbers are satisfied with a little bit and leave as quickly as they came.

Hearing about Brazilian robberies reminds of the stories I heard in the seventies and eighties about going to New York. They would tell you to always take twenty dollars with you so that in case you were mugged, you would have something to give the robber. The implication was if you had that twenty dollars to hand over, you would be fine and it would be over within seconds. If not or if you resisted, you might get hurt or worse. It seems to me that this is how the Brazilians look at robberies today.

Using a money belt or belly band is can be a good idea, but they are somewhat uncomfortable, especially in the hot climates such as Brazil. That said, they do work most of the time. I used a slightly different technique that was recommended to me by my guide. I carried two wallets and two telephones. I left my nice jewelry and watch at home. The thought was to have an inexpensive phone, watch and a wallet with a small amount of cash, receipts, etc. to give to your thief. I either carried all of them in my front pockets or if I was going somewhere that I felt very safe in, I would put the disposable ones in my back pockets.

Along the same lines, do not wear expensive or important jewelry. Do not wear your nicest watch, necklace, ear rings or rings. The best advice is to leave them at home in a shirt pocket hanging in the closet or some other fairly safe place. The thieves at home will take the safe and jewelry boxes first so don't put them there. Unfortunately that is a fact I learned when one of my past homes in the U.S. was broken into and robbed.

If you are robbed in Brazil, don't hesitate to give the thieves your disposable phone, wallet, watch and whatever cheap jewelry you have on. After talking it over with my guide, I did wear my wedding ring and a religious necklace. She informed me that most thieves will respect the sanctity of these two items only. If you feel you need to give up your other phone and wallet to remain safe, do it and know it's a smart decision. Stuff is just stuff. Your life or the ones with you are always more important than stuff.

Do not speak, especially English or gringo Portuguese if you can avoid it. Let your guide or Portuguese speaking friends handle the talking. If the thieves think you're a rich tourist, you could be taking a ride around to several ATMs or even kidnapped for ransom. Both of these situations are rarer than a simple robbery, but are not totally unheard of in most countries. I am not sure if running after you hand over your stuff is a good idea or not.

My thoughts were to react based on the specific situation at the time. If I was alone with no one to speak, I would probably run or fight. If with others, probably not, but if it seemed like a hostage situation might occur, I think I would try to put up a good fight and take my chances right there. Fighting a robber seems to be unheard of in Brazil. Whether it is the New York mugging mentality, their culture or Brazilians just considering themselves lovers and not fighters or something entirely different, I don't know.

Remember, be a boy scout, be ready and think about how you will handle situations before they occur. If you are with others, talk to them about their thoughts and express your plans. For those Americans that exercise their second amendment rights when home, guns are illegal to own, let alone carry in Brazil. Remember only the bad guys, guards and the military are armed and sometimes the police. I am pretty sure they would just throw a gringo under the jail if he were caught with a firearm. Don't forget rule number one, pay attention to your surroundings and the people paying attention to you.

I will attempt a brief summary of Brazil as seen through a gringo's eyes. It is amazingly beautiful in so many places and ways, especially the natural beauty of the land and seascapes and ugly in only a few. It is mostly old, but some areas are so modern they almost seem futuristic. It can be like stepping back in time thirty, forty, fifty years or more and then you cross the street and it as modern as any U.S. city today. I have kidded my guide many times that Brazil is a first, second and third world country all rolled up into one, but sincerely it seems that way to me.

A large part of the population is poor and the middle class seems small. Doctors, lawyers and other college educated professionals are mostly part of the middle class, instead of the rich. Corruption seems to be accepted or at least not as sugar coated as it is in the U.S. and more out in the open. Brazil is a little wilder than I am accustomed to. It makes me think of several older and wilder time periods in the U.S. that coexist all at the same time here.

As with every other place I have traveled, the over whelming majority of people are good folks that welcome visitors and try to help. The Brazilians I know are absolutely wonderful, generous to a fault, fun loving and welcoming in every way. Don't wait to have your adventure of a lifetime in Brazil, do it now and you won't regret it.

# ABOUT THE AUTHOR

I am an over fifty American who loves to travel and explore. I am lucky enough to have good friends and an amazing family who have always supported my adventures. Surprise, my Brazilian guide is also my lovely and talented wife, along with being the co-editor of this book. We plan to continue traveling, exploring and making new friends in as many places as we can.

I hope you have enjoyed this book and it helps make your first trip to Brazil marvelous. If you thought it was helpful or entertaining, please recommend it to your friends and family and consider giving us a positive review. If not, please forget you ever read our book and don't worry about that review thing.

More at Amazon.com or NeededKnowledge.com

# OTHER BOOKS BY JF LEWIS

Travel Made Easy Series, Volume 1"Gringo in Brazil, Quick Guide for Enjoying Brazil on Your First Trip Plus a Little Portuguese the Easy Way"

This was our first, but not last book. Number two is well on its way.

Thank you for reading our book and please review it on Amazon if you enjoyed it, thought it was helpful or you at least got a few good chuckles from it.

To all of our friends and family at home and abroad, thank you so very much for your help, support, generosity and friendship.

Tchau Beijos and God bless!

0 1341 1366917 7